STOP Rejection:
Simple Tips for Becoming a DATING Champion
(Body Language WORKS !)

I0439286

TABLE OF CONTENTS

Dating Champion in 1-2-3

Nothing will prepare you for becoming a dating champion like a keen understanding of body language. The body is one of the greatest communication tools that has ever existed, and it is also the least understood. When people develop knowledge of this unspoken language and a talent for using and interpreting it, they can avoid rejection every time.

Your own body language can make you more appealing to others. This happens when people start perceiving you as a warm, inviting, and honest person just by how you position yourself and your receptive responses as an audience. People love being listened to and made to feel as though they are the center of attention. You can train your physical self to provide this response, ensuring that you leave a trail of admirers wherever you go.

Using good body language is one of the fastest and most effective ways to convince others that you are worth their time and attention. This is why sales people from all over the world spend countless hours learning how to portray a strong, confident image and why politicians are diligent and careful in their every physical move. Before a person utters a single word, his or her posture will have already given out an unlimited amount of information. By calculating these revelations, politicians, salespeople, and others can be sure that the most beneficial messages are always conveyed.

People who are experienced in reading body language and those who have no experience at all are both able to pick up on the many subtle and unconscious clues that others send. This means that it is possible to turn a love interest entirely off even before you cross the room or open your mouth. It is also possible to drive this same person mad with desire, by simply choosing to use your body differently.

Tip #1– Be mindful of your body. You are communicating important messages to others even when you are not trying to. If you are careful in the construction of these physical messages, you can always make a good impression.

There are many other reasons why learning the secrets of body language is so important. When you can discern the emotions of others without having to ask how they are feeling, you can assess your dating opportunities early and easily. You can determine whether or not a person is interested, on the verge of experiencing interest, or will never exhibit any interest at all. This is one of the greatest advantages you can gain from this newfound understanding because it means that you may never have to face rejection again and that you can always be sure to pick up on the signs of a growing attraction, well before the other person has made his or her own daring approach.

You can also use your body language to turn people down easily. There are many different clues you can exhibit that will help a person understand that you are closed off to his or her advances. Rather than engaging in hurtful or awkward conversations, you can avoid unwanted approaches by simply conveying your disinterest with your body.

Ultimately, learning about body language can have a very dramatic impact on your view of the world and the people who live in it. Communication does not spring from the mouth alone. People are constantly transmitting signals to one another without being verbal at all. Discovering these signals and their inherent meanings will help you to navigate the social scene deftly and with passion, purpose, and a clear understanding of how to get what you really want.

CHAPTER 1
BODY LANGUAGE

1.1 What is Body Language?

Body language is a non-verbal way that people communicate with one another. Gestures, posture, and even the physical distance that people put between themselves and others can convey a lot. Learning how to interpret this method of communication and how to effectively send out the right signals is vital for dating success. When you learn how to use your body to transmit seductive or romantic messages to others, you do not have to worry about choosing the right words or stumbling over your sentences.

More importantly, as you become adept in reading the signals of others, you will be able to spot potential rejections and budding interest from a mile away. The simple act of reading a person's physical language can help you avoid engaging in unnecessary conversations, while showing you how to make the most of opportunities with prospective dating prospects. You do not have to be a body language expert to learn these subtle techniques. In fact, most people have been reading these signals and using them for years, without even knowing it.

For instance, when you find yourself annoyed with someone, you probably find that your body naturally turns away from that individual. You make little eye contact and few affirmative gestures when he or she speaks. You probably find it difficult to smile, especially genuinely.

This is your natural way of conveying your desire to either get away from this person or have the unwanted conversation come to an end. Much of body language and how it is used is instinctive. In many ways, it can be considered an unconscious method of conveying true feelings without ever uttering a single word. In this sense, body language can trump verbal efforts at expression. While a person might verbally commit to remaining in an unwanted conversation, his or her body language is certain to say otherwise.

In many instances, gestures or postures can imply that a person is closed off from the conversation without rejecting the actual speaker. Rather than turning away, the individual is using his or her arms or shoulders to reject the message instead. For example, an audience might cross the arms over the body to suggest that he or she does not like the topic of conversation or the direction it is taking. Although this person is not engaged with the words of the speaker, if he or she has not turned away from the speaker, this is likely a rejection of the actual message, rather than a rejection of the person who is delivering it. The subtle differences in positioning and movement can mean a lot, and the ability to pick up on these things will give you a lot more understanding of the dating arena.

Tip #2 – Be careful not to interpret a rejection of your words as a rejection of you personally. Your audience might not like the direction the conversation is taking, but could be interested in talking with you more about other things.

It is important to note that body language can also be very culturally influenced, which makes it necessary to ascertain any major differences that lie between yourself and your audience or the person whose body language you are attempting to read. Different cultures will use their bodies in different ways to close off conversation, reject speakers, or warmly invite them in.

Two Main Types

There are ultimately two types of body language: OPEN and CLOSED.

With open body language, you are using your physicality to show others that you are open to interacting with them. This is generally done by looking directly into the eyes of the individual who is speaking. You do not cross your legs, fold your arms, or cover any parts of your body or attempt to hide them. One example of hiding might be to close or cover the palms or entire hands. This can be done by shoving your hands into your pockets or sitting on them. Any of these activities, whether purposefully or inadvertently performed, can suggest an inner intention to close the personal self off from the speaker.

Closed body language is easy to interpret, even for those who are not experienced in determining the inherent meanings of posturing or physical movements. These are actions like turning away, avoiding eye contact, or crossing the arms. These actions are commonly known to suggest disinterest or a dedicated effort to distract attention or avert it to someone else. People can use outside barriers to avert attention or suggest apprehension as well. For instance, a concerted effort to sit with a table, shelf, or any other physical item between you and the speaker shows a deliberate attempt to avoid physical contact or closeness of any type. Hence, if you are attempting to make a romantic advance on someone and he or she chooses to sit far away from you with a physical barrier between you, the advance is probably an unwanted one.

Tip #3 – Never cross your arms over your body when engaged in conversation. This lets the speaker know that you are not receptive to what he or she is saying and can make you seem unapproachable.

1.2 Change Yourself (Using Your Body Language)

It is impossible to affect an attitude that you do not truly believe in, all the time. Holding your head high and squaring your shoulders can make you appear more confident to the untrained eye; however, there will be unconscious signals that you are likely to send that will show signs of nervousness, fear of failure, and inner apprehension. Studies have shown, however, that the act of consciously controlling your body language in order to display a greater level of confidence can actually help you to develop a stronger belief in your own growing confidence. Thus, you really can fake it until you make it.

This is something that you must keep in mind when working to transition from closed body language to open forms of body language. Those who are open tend to appear more confident than those who are continually closed off. Rather than letting low self-esteem or social apprehension prevent you from reaching out, start pretending to be the engaging and personable individual you really want to be.

Tip #4 – Start making an effort to maintain good posture at all times. Sitting or standing with your spine straight and your head held high will make you look more interesting and lively. You will start feeling that way too.

1.3 The Power Of Body Language

Body language helps people feel accepted, interesting, and worthy of attention. Assuming the wrong posture when playing audience to a romantic interest can make the person feel less than important. When you turn your body toward a speaker, make good eye contact, and use your hands and arms to convey your interest, you can become more captivating and pleasant to be around. In every culture and at every age, people enjoy being listened to and taken seriously. People tend to gravitate toward individuals who make them feel appreciated and worth paying attention to.

Unfortunately, most people go through life without ever learning how to use their bodies effectively. They do not know how to make their desire known or how to convey an attitude of confidence and self-assurance. Instead, these individuals play victim to their bodies and let their own subconscious minds rule how they are postured and how they use their limbs. Ultimately, what they are doing is letting their subconscious movements determine how others will perceive them, receive them, and respond to them.

When you make a conscious effort to control your body and use it as a valuable part of the communication process, you will have a lot more control over the results you get when speaking to others. You can show people that you want to hear more of what they have to say or that you want to get to know them better or even a little more intimately. Best of all, as you grow more skilled in your ability to use your physicality as an effective communication device, you will also become equally skilled in interpreting the physical communication of others.

Tip #5 – Listen actively and always make good eye contact. People listen to others all day long, but rarely feel as though they are being actively listened to. You can stand out in the minds of dating prospects by simply being someone who is considerate enough to pay attention.

In dating, body language can mean the difference between getting dates and not getting dates. The right movements and stances can help you progress to new levels of physical intimacy, just as the wrong ones can get you shut out of the boudoir forever. Ultimately, this is an extraordinarily powerful communication tool and one that people use whether they recognize it or not.

Impact of the Absence of Body Language

The true power of body language is most easily recognized in its absence. People can have a frightful time discerning the underlying meaning of words and phrases that are sent via email, text messages, and SMS. The ambiguity of spoken or written words is made horribly apparent when there is no physical basis for determining the actual intentions behind them.

A text can mean anything when sent from person to person and might appear to convey honest communication or an attempt at sarcasm or wry humor. The fear of making a wrongful interpretation can be present both when sending and receiving communications that are absent of body language. Intended emotions can be more easily known when the audience has the opportunity to read the facial expressions of the message sender or recipient and to analyze his or her body language. Thus, in many ways body language is a powerful key for deciphering the true intentions of a speaker and the ultimate response of the audience. When it is absent, people often find themselves wandering in the dark, only able to guess at what the speaker's or recipient's true emotions really are.

1.4 Body Language Signs

There are a number of tell-tale body language signs that make it far easier for people to decipher this manner of communicating. The study of body language is vast, but with a bit of insight, anyone can learn how to use this tool to gain the affections of a long sought-after love interest or increase the likelihood of new intimacy. The following are a few subtle hints that both men and women can send that show whether they are interested or disinterested in their audiences.

1.4.1 Facial Expressions

In his 1872 book, *The Expressions of the Emotions in Man and Animals*, Charles Darwin asserted that there are certain facial expressions that are universal in both their meaning and interpretation. This best-selling book had a vast and highly controversial appeal and remains an accepted manual for defining and interpreting facial expressions in humans. The gist of this publication was that man is universally capable of expressing six expressions with the musculature and features of the face alone, these being fear, sadness, happiness, anger, surprise, and distrust.

The idea is that no matter where you go or which culture you are communicating in, the facial conveyance of these emotions will always be the same. When you think of it, these are emotions that you can easily recognize in others and which you probably assign to certain common facial movements. Wide eyes and a slack, surprised jaw generally mean that a person is afraid or has been caught off guard. A genuine smile always means happiness and interest, unless it is performed in such a way as to become a sneer. Cinched lips and a furrowed brow connote anger, and a smirk is commonly associated with distrust.

Understanding this, you can see that you are already well adept in reading some forms of body language, even if these forms are totally restricted to the face. When people use their faces to either consciously or subconsciously transmit messages, it becomes a lot easier for others to know what they are feeling without the addition of words. You are probably less familiar with the use of the body to convey feelings of sexual tension, regret, desire, or other emotions that apply directly to the dating game. Learning how to read these things, however, can become just as second nature as reading emotions via facial expressions.

1.4.2 Eyebrow Movements

A quick upward movement of the eyebrows can connote attraction in both men and women. This does not last long and is usually not a very dramatic movement. It is an unconscious gesture that both sexes commonly make when they are in the presence of someone they find particularly appealing.

Look for quick upward movement of the eyebrows, as it might indicate that the person finds you very attractive.

1.4.3 A Slightly Open Mouth

Men and women will also open their mouths slightly when in the presence of a partner or prospective mate they find attractive. This is a purely sexual gesture and one that implies a generous amount of physical desire. This will typically take place when two people make eye contact.

While making eye contact, look for an open mouth. If it's there, there might be physical/sexual attraction in the game.

1.4.4 The Direction of the Knees and Toes

How people position their legs and feet is a clear indicator of physical desire or strong interest. If a person is talking to you with his or her toes pointed toward you, there is a definite interest in further communication. Turning the toes away and letting the shoulders follow is a sign of disinterest and could indicate that the person is closed off or wants the conversation to end.

Another sure sign of sexual attraction is when a woman sits with her legs crossed and folded beneath her and her knees pointing toward you. This is an unconscious conveyance of an inner wish for you to take decisive action and make an aggressive approach. Crossing and uncrossing the legs can be a more aggressive and conscious way for a woman to show interest in physical intimacy.

1.4.5 Playing With the Hair

Women tend to move their hair away from their faces in order to show their attention, sympathy, affection, or interest in a man. Her efforts to adjust or fix her hair while talking to a prospective partner show that she is concerned with her appearance. The nature of these movements can connote nervousness or insecurity, but in most instances, movements that involve the hair do depict a sincere interest in the male audience.

Men tend to do a lot of fidgeting with their hair when in the presence of a romantic interest as well. They may smooth their hair down or fluff it up. This too is an act of preening or a subconscious attempt to enhance the appearance. Women enjoy watching these attempts to spruce up as they are an obvious and easy-to-read show of interest.

1.4.6 Facial Touching

Touching the face can mean many things; however, when the hands stray near the mouth while talking, this is often a signal that the individual is not telling the whole truth. This is especially true when men start fidgeting with their chins, cheeks, and ears while making sexual or romantic advances. They may be trying to determine the best way of presenting themselves in a positive light without stretching the truth too far. They might also be covering up their current dating status or their true intentions for hooking up.

Hand movement around the face is a combination of autoerotic action and nervousness or tension. Touching the cheeks or chin is usually an unconscious movement, and these actions are commonly believed to be rooted in sexual desire. Anything that is done with the mouth while speaking, whether smoking or drinking, is likely to increase in frequency when one person is attracted to another. People will take more sips from their cups and more drags from their cigarettes, and these things, too, are signs of romantic interest.

1.4.7 Handling Phallus-Shaped Objects

Holding, touching, or manually manipulating cylindrical or phallus-shaped objects is something that is both subconsciously and consciously done. When females or gay men want to send direct body signals that they are interested in a sexual advance, holding or handling a phallus-shaped object is one of the easiest ways to do so. Subconsciously, however, straight men will do this as well, as the phallus is commonly thought to represent the female breasts. These actions can be as simple as playing with a straw or a tall drinking glass. Women will also work harder to keep their wrists and palms visible to their male audiences when they are attracted to them.

1.4.8 Making Clothing Adjustments

Clothing adjustments can convey a variety of emotions. Pulling an open blouse closed at the neckline can show apprehension, distrust, or a desire to appear more modest. Adjusting the hemline of the skirt so that it falls closer to the knees is another action a woman might take when being pursued by an unwanted aggressor. These are closed signals that women commonly send before issuing a verbal rejection.

Men tend to preen when they are interested and will adjust their ties in an attempt to draw more attention to them. Fixing their lapels or adjusting their shirts shows the same intentions. When a man removes his coat and places his hands on his hips, he is already ready to conquer. Conversely, when he points his toes directly away from his female audience, he has already lost interest.

1.4.9 Offering a Guiding Hand

The hand that guides is another common sign of male affection. Men who gently place their hands on the arms, lower backs, or across the shoulders of a woman while walking or standing are showing a public sign of affection and possession. They are attempting to act as guides, and this leadership position is also an effort to show dominance.

1.5 Decoding Body Language

Now that you know that body language is real, identifiable, and distinguishable, you might be wondering whether or not there is a simple way to interpret body language every time. The answer to this is, of course, no. There are simply too many variables that must be factored into the equation. These include cultural differences, the speaker's level of cognizant awareness of body language, and your own intuition when it comes to picking up on common signals.

You can, however, become better at recognizing key signs of interest and disinterest. You can learn when to determine whether people are telling the truth and when they are lying. You can also learn to determine when someone is making sexual advances and when they want you to start making sexual advances of your own.

The clues that will help you to do so are actually very simple. In fact, they can be glaringly obvious in many instances. This is because many of these clues are associated with facial features or movements of the face.

Lying

A liar cannot help but to exhibit tell-tale signs of the prevarication that is brewing. For instance, a person who is telling a lie is likely to touch his or her mouth frequently while talking. Many experts suggest that this is an unconscious effort to brush the untruth away. He or she might also wink while talking and will often touch his or her nose as well. Studies have shown that people who are under stress while talking are also likely to purse the lips.

Tip #7 – Be cautious about touching the face while answering questions about yourself. This is a common and well-known sign that someone is telling an untruth. It is also an impulse reaction for men and women who are slightly aroused. Given the dramatic differences in these two messages, it is best to keep your hands down and visible when discussing important subjects.

Sexual Attraction

The signs of sexual attraction are quite a bit more familiar to most than the signs of lying. This body language is so easy to detect and so clearly conveys the intentions of the individual that it is used in advertising campaigns across the world. People watch others use body language to flirt and transmit sexual messages via television commercials and even print ad campaigns. The ways in which men and women hold their bodies, position themselves toward one another, and display the hands, are all cues that can help you to determine whether or not someone is sending subtle signals for a passionate advance.

1.6 Why You Should Be Using Body Language

The question of whether or not to use body language is a moot one. It is physically impossible not to communicate with your body without investing a tremendous amount of effort. Even then, your body will continue to send out a range of unconscious signs and messages that connote and define your moods and intentions. In fact, most would agree that it is easier to consciously control your body language than it is to eliminate any messages, whether subtle or blatant, from your alternative methods of communicating. People find it hard not to gesticulate when they talk, while others find it impossible not to slouch or turn away when they are bored. Consciously directing your movements, however, helps you to conceal less-than-positive reactions while broadcasting amorous affections or romantic intentions.

For instance, you can learn to hold your body alert and erect while others are speaking, even if you do not like what they are saying. Your posture and the way in which you move your eyes and hold your torso can show your interest, even if the interest is only feigned. Although there are a number of ways to fake specific types of body language in order to deliver an intended message, it is important to know that there is no way to control all movements and all signals that are sent. You will both convey the intended message and transmit a variety of signals that you are not aware of, whether these are nervous gestures or other postures or movements that belie your actual emotions. Thus, even though you can pretend to be more confident by standing fully erect and making direct contact, you will not be able to fool everyone with these efforts.

Becoming a More Interesting and Engaging Person

All you need to do is simply think back to some of the crowded rooms you have entered in the past to learn how effective body language can be. There were likely people who sat with their knees turned away from their audiences and their arms folded in. People who keep their heads down and their bodies closed tend to be a lot less intriguing than those who offer a very open body and who communicate with their physical selves in a very engaging way.

Odds are that the very first people you attempt to communicate with in circumstances like these are the very people who are first to make eye contact, the first to turn their bodies toward you, and the first to welcome you in with a motion, a gesture, or even their posture. It is the inherent fear of rejection that all people have that makes them assess the silent communication that people are constantly transmitting before reaching out.

If you become the person in the room who is consciously transmitting an open signal, more people will reach out to you and engage. This is how people become the star of the room. They are attentive audiences and are welcoming in their every move. Their very presence helps others to feel more confident, assured, and worthy. Thus, by simply learning how to use your body in the right way, you can make yourself more interesting to the people around you, whether they have known you for a while or are just meeting you for the very first time.

Tip #8 – Picture yourself extending your heart to the people you most want to meet. With your shoulders drawn back, you will be less likely to slouch over and will be physically displaying the signs of an OPEN personality. Good body language starts with good posture.

Boost Your Own Self-Esteem

It cannot be stated enough that it is possible to fake confidence on some levels until you are able to build enough confidence on your own to no longer need to focus on your own body signals with great diligence. The simple act of pulling your shoulders back, holding your head high, and acting as though you are in possession of a great and powerful sense of self-assurance will make you seem more impressive and dominant to others. With time, you will naturally begin to mimic the emotions that your own body language conveys. People who let their shoulders slump inward and their heads hang low will ultimately do the same. In essence, how you hold your body, move it, position it, and communicate with it will often determine how you feel about yourself. Making an effort consciously tailors your posturing to suggest the very emotions that you hope to feel will usually help you to attain these emotions over time.

Become More Dominant and Proactive

As your own body language conditions you to feel more optimal, you will also begin to perform more optimally. People who feel confident do more, and these are also the same individuals who naturally invite more people in. As your social circle expands, your ability to deal with this larger audience and the necessary confidence for this level of entertaining will naturally follow.

Tip #9 – Recognize that courage is not fearlessness. Courageous people are often afraid, but they continue to act in spite of their fears. This is also true of confidence. Opening yourself up to a room of new people might seem intimidating, but even the social butterflies in your circle are not immune to getting butterflies of their own. Thus, act like you are courageous and confident even when you do not feel that way. With time, you will be both of these things.

Treating Body Language Like a Hobby

The best stage performers are aware of the undeniable power and importance of body language. These are the best actors and dancers. They know how to use every fiber of their beings to create and display emotions. If you want to enhance your art, learning how to use and interpret body language will play a very vital role in doing so. It is impossible to convince people that you are feeling any specific emotion if you cannot train your body to convey it first. Voice and inflection alone will not convince your audience. With the proper body language, however, you can actually become the very characters that you are called upon to portray.

1.7 How to Adapt and Change Your Body Language

As with all things in life, practice makes perfect when it comes to good use of body language. The more you train yourself to respond to certain social circumstances with the appropriate physical response, the more second nature and natural these responses will become. This is the key to being convincing when attempting to consciously control actions that are primarily rooted in the subconscious.

In dating, the rules are a lot easier to bend, as people from both genders are constantly trying to communicate hidden feelings without speaking them outright. Thus, if you do not want your gestures or postures to seem affected, you will simply need to give yourself time to perfect them through practice. Small, subtle clues like positioning your feet toward the target of your affections are not as easy for people to read.

Tip #10 – Avoid facing or looking at the door while engaged in conversation. Doing so makes it look like you want to get away.

You cannot assume that others will be working to develop the same level of understanding about the body and how it works in silent communication. Thus, responses that are generally issued from the limbic part of the brain will usually only be effective on people who understand limbic brain activity and the physical responses that it is likely to generate. You will have to be a little bit more forthright in physical flirting of this type.

People will definitely respond better to your attempts to be more open and welcoming by using OPEN body language. With romantic interests, however, you can engage in more amorous displays of your affections by playing with your hair intentionally, adjusting your clothing suggestively, and positioning yourself closer to the other party. These aggressive and hard-to-miss movements will allow you to carefully assess the response of your audience. Timing is key, as moving too fast can easily result in an equally fast rejection. By taking it slow, you can calculate the effects of your movements and use the resulting information to determine whether or not you should continue your pursuit, take it slow, or leave off entirely.

CHAPTER 2
DATING

2.1 The Power of Attraction

It is impossible to discuss the power of attraction without addressing how it influences body language. When a person is attracted to another individual, his or her physical self will appear to be almost drawn to the other party, much like a magnet. For instance, the feet and shoulders will turn in, the eyes will gravitate in their direction, and, in many instances, the limbic brain will cause the attracted party to unconsciously mimic his or her movements, even if only in a very modest fashion. If the subject touches his or her hair, the admirer will quickly follow suit. If the subject moistens or opens his or her mouth, the admirer will inadvertently do the same.

It is difficult to check these unconscious motions, as they arise without thought or will and often without the notice of the person who is making them. In fact, when the power of attraction rears its head, people are not generally thinking with the portion of the brain that allows them to be aware of their motions. These things are subtle signals that are sent by the brain and conveyed by physical language to the other party as a very primitive way of gaining their sought-after attention. People actually start flirting long before they intend to.

Even a very simple thing, like a warm, welcome smile, is a very blatant yet unconscious way to show interest. Although the smile is a universal sign of happiness, it is also a universal way of appreciating the presence or company of someone else. A smile can be faked or issued at whim; however, those that arise unbidden when a person is attracted to another are genuine, delightful, and personally joyous experiences. Smiles like these truly show how physical motions and facial expressions can make a person feel the very same emotions that the body is conveying. The very recognition of this type of smile often makes the person feel giddy and smile wider.

2.2 Sexual Attraction

Learning when to make sexual advances and when to hold off is the key to avoiding rejection. There are few people in the world who are eager to face rejection, which makes it a tremendous relief to discover that there are very effective ways for determining when a sexual invitation is being offered, when it is being withdrawn, and when it is going to be accepted. A lot of these cues are transmitted subconsciously; however, some are well thought out and sent with a very clear intent.

How Men Let You Know That They Are Ready to Be Intimate

When it comes to sex, men can be a lot more verbally aggressive than women, especially with new partners. This is due in large part to the fact that this is behavior that is viewed as being more socially acceptable in men than in women, as long as it is done within reason. Because of this, men tend to use body language in this area more as an effort to make themselves seem more physically impressive and dominant.

A man might stand taller and square his shoulders or pull them back. Puffing out his chest and holding his head high are other unconscious signals that he might send out. These are things that are done to make his frame appear larger and more masculine. A man might even square his jaw as a sign of dominance. Men will also pull their abdomens in to look sleeker.

How Women Let You Know That They Are Ready to Physically Engage

For women, approaching sex in a verbal fashion has long been considered to be a bit more taboo. Although the gender rules of several decades ago no longer apply, females in certain cultures are held to a different sexual standard than men, making it much more necessary for women to reveal their desires and intentions through physical clues and subtleties. The line between conscious and unconscious body language can therefore be considered to be a bit blurred, especially given that many of the same signals are sent whether or not the woman is cognizant of her own movements or actions.

A woman will always point her feet toward the man that she is interested in. She will show her palms and wrists at all times. Her mouth will hang slightly open and she will become fixated on wetting or licking her lips or rubbing her lips together. She might caress her own neck or arms in a show of her more subtle erogenous zones.

It is important to remember the basic and easy to discern difference between OPEN and CLOSED forms of body language. If a person appears open to your advances, this is a sure sign that your advances are appreciated. If there are movements to cross the arms or legs, however, or to point the feet or turn the shoulders away from you, this individual is closing off your advances and does not want you to continue your approach.

Tip #11 – Take your time. If you are using body language as a way to gauge someone else's sexual mood, make sure to inch your way closer rather than to dive right into your love interest's lap. This will give you ample opportunity to assess the physical responses that are issued as you close the distance. Firm and unwavering eye contact will make your advances impossible to ignore.

You should always keep in mind that body language is but one manner of communicating. The verbal response always trumps any message that the body is transmitting during a sexual pursuit. Thus, while the target of your affections might be sending every physical clue that he or she is ready to actively engage in a passionate encounter, a verbal denial of these things should generally cause you to back off. When a person invites you verbally but denies your advance through body language, there can be a number of reasons for this mixed message, and you have to follow the verbal encouragement of a prospective partner according to your own comfort level. This can be an extremely uncomfortable position to be in and one that you are not obligated to keep yourself in beyond your ability to tolerate or enjoy it.

2.3 When to Stop Trying

You have to know when to stop trying after having done all that you can to transmit the right signals. If you are constantly pursuing someone who is eager to back away from you, turn away from you in conversation, or perpetually keep his or her arms crossed, you are essentially pursuing a dead end. The signs of CLOSED body language ultimately mean that a person is closed off.

It is important to note that closed signals are not always something that should be taken personally. Instead, they could be a sign that the target of your affections already has a partner, is in the middle of reconnecting with a former partner, or has other obligations or obstacles in life that are not permitting openness at the present moment. While closed body signals are a rejection of the offer to date or be intimate, they do not always mean a direct objection to you. They can very well mean a rejection of the offer itself for a variety of non-personal reasons, even though their body language has not changed.

A person may or may not become verbal about his or her lack of desire for further pursuit, especially when your own body signals become hard to ignore. If you are pursuing someone aggressively and using your best efforts to convey interest through your posture and stance, it is best to back down when these efforts do not win you the results you are seeking after any considerable amount of time. This is especially true if they continue to earn you closed body signals in response. A failure to back down will usually earn you a verbal rejection, which can be a lot more damaging to the ego.

Tip #12 – Always be a good sport about rejection. Someone who turns you down today could introduce you to a friend or associate tomorrow who might be just right for you.

2.4 Notes for Gay People

Learning how to read body language can be a bit more complex for gay people, as there are dramatic differences in how people communicate sexual attraction in same-sex relationships or interactions. There are new variables and different barriers that must be hurdled, especially in instances in which people may or may not be upfront or comfortable with their sexual identities. Avoiding rejection is just as important for gay and lesbian individuals, if not more so, as these individuals are not just reaching out to engage with others but are effectively inquiring about individuals' sexual identities as well.

Gay men have a number of things they will often do in order to make a sexual advance known. As with straight men, these signals are just as much subconsciously constructed as consciously. For instance, a man will pull his shoulders back, puff his chest out, and stretch his head taller when pursuing another male. These are the common signs of male dominance and they do not vary according to sexual preference. Men will again square their jaws to show their dominance and are always likely to draw the abdomen in to provide a sleeker and more appealing physique. These are usually quick changes in posturing that are quickly enacted and easy to notice.

In the dating world, many things do not differ when it comes to straight male body language and gay male body language. Men tend to point their feet and shoulders toward their object of interest whether they are pursuing a male or a female partner. They tend to make good eye contact and focus intently when being spoken to. If no interest exists, they will exhibit the signs of closure by turning their feet and bodies away, limiting eye contact, and smiling less often. It is important to note, however, that gay men tend to be more aggressive and forthright in their physical pursuits in order to leave behind any confusion about sexual orientation or intention.

For lesbian women there can be marked differences. Studies have shown that lesbian women tend to pay greater attention to voice pitch, tonality, and physical actions than they do actual words. They look more intently for physical clues and signs of responsiveness. Thus, when lesbian women are reaching out, they must take special care to avoid sending signals that show they are closed off. They should hold themselves erect and with confidence and focus on making a prospective love interest feel welcome, invited, and comfortable by carefully positioning their bodies toward their audiences and suggesting that they are captivated by the speaker.

CHAPTER 3
Case Study: Getting Ready to
Conquer in Love and Passion

Cathy is a twenty-four year old woman who has not been on a date in six months. She is extremely attracted to the bartender at a local haunt that she and her friends often visit. His name is Greg and he is handsome, physically fit, and single.

Deciding that she will make her move when she next sees him, she makes a dedicated effort to dress the part of the single and highly available woman that she is. Upon entering the room, she focuses on keeping her shoulders pulled back, her head held high, and her smile easy. She of course points her toes in the direction of Greg and keeps them there, holding his eyes once she gets his attention.

The goal of her approach is little more than to have a heated physical experience with the hot body who pours drinks for her and her pals. She knows that the likelihood of a long-term romance is limited, given his massive popularity and his young and free-willed spirit. More importantly, she knows that she is not yet ready for any major commitment herself.

She sits directly across from him and smiles. It is a welcoming and warm smile, one that surely outshines all of the other swooning females that line the bar. When he slides her a drink, she handles the straw suggestively while using her other hand to push her hair away from her face. She keeps her hands visible, her palms open and loose, and when she is not sipping away at her beverage she keeps her mouth slightly ajar and moistens her lips from time to time.

All the while she is watching Greg's movements and being careful to make her watching obvious. When he moves, she purses her lips with satisfaction and raises her eyebrows ever so slightly. He is sending the right signals as well. He watches her watching him, and when his work will allow it, he turns to give her an appreciative smile, a lingering stare, and a full-on view of his massive physique.

When at last they speak, their intentions are already entirely clear. There is no need to shout over the music or make small talk. She has not been sending subtle innuendos but blaring cries of her desire, and Greg has matched her in his responsiveness. He touches her hand, and she does not pull away but leans into him, reaching with her torso by bending across the bar. She adjusts her shirt and again brushes her hair.

"I close up at 2," he says.

"I'll see you then," she replies. And this is all that either of them must say.

Conclusion

Once you have learned how to use your body language to transmit a clear and easily identifiable message of your romantic or sexual interest in others, you will be far more likely to start getting the responses you want. Your knowledge and experience with this manner of communicating will help you to identify interested and willing dating prospects and subtly encourage their own approaches.

One of the most difficult aspects of dating is determining what people are feeling, what they want, and when you have crossed an important comfort zone or barrier. The very act of reading and deciphering body language can help you to progress from the formative stages of a relationship into levels of deep physical intimacy without offending your partner, overstepping boundaries, or turning him or her off.

Best of all, your newfound understanding will make you a better, more confident, and more approachable person in other areas of life. You can condition your body to affect the very way in which you perceive yourself. By believing yourself to be more confident and carrying yourself more confidently, you can actually become more self-assured.

These techniques will allow you to improve your life in every way by helping you to become the open, engaging, and interesting person you are meant to be. Instead of suffering rejection and the pitfalls of dating misunderstandings, you can start reaching out to people who really want to be with you and who are eagerly awaiting your advances. You can also use your body language to enhance this interest and start putting out a more attractive image that draws the kind of dating prospects you really want to have.

There are many ways to communicate; however, non-verbal communication through the use of physical posturing and movements is the most important of them. People use and interpret body language every day. If you have not learned how to do so, you are not only missing out, but you are cheating yourself. This is true in the social scene and in your professional and private life.

Bonus: Checklist

Thanks a lot for reading this book. If you like this book, please leave me a review on Amazon.

Moreover, quick action takers get rewarded!

Get your bonus using this URL: http://eepurl.com/sTFpn, and

1. Receive useful references for further reading.
2. Get a PDF checklist of the twelve tips.
3. Get my next book on Amazon for FREE!